HOW IT WORKS

HOW IT WORKS

DANIEL MACIVOR

How It Works
first published 2006 by
Scirocco Drama
An imprint of J. Gordon Shillingford Publishing Inc.
© 2006 Daniel MacIvor
Reprinted October 2007

Scirocco Drama Editor: Glenda MacFarlane
Cover design by Terry Gallagher/Doowah Design Inc.
Author photo by Guntar Kravis
Printed and bound in Canada

We acknowledge the financial support of the Manitoba Arts Council, The Canada
Council for the Arts and the Government of Canada through the Book Publishing
Industry Development Program (BPIDP) for our publishing program.

Library and Archives Canada Cataloguing in Publication

MacIvor, Daniel, 1962-
How it works/Daniel MacIvor.

A play.
ISBN 1-897289-07-3

I. Title.

PS8575.I86H69 2006   C812'.54   C2006-902986-5

J. Gordon Shillingford Publishing
P.O. Box 86, RPO Corydon Avenue, Winnipeg, MB Canada R3M 3S3

For Paul Goulet

Daniel MacIvor

Daniel MacIvor was born in Cape Breton, Nova Scotia in 1962. He has been creating new theatre since 1986 and was for twenty years Artistic Director of da da kamera, an international touring company based in Toronto which helped change the way theatre is developed in Canada. His published work includes: *See Bob Run, Never Swim Alone, House/Humans, Monster* (Scirocco Drama), *Here Lies Henry, You Are Here* (Scirocco Drama), *In On It* (Scirocco Drama), and *I Still Love You: Five Plays*. He works with theatres across Canada and the United States including New York's Urbanstages and Nova Scotia's Mulgrave Road Theatre. He has been the recipient of several Dora Mavor Moore Awards, two Chalmers Awards, and an Obie Award. Also a filmmaker, he has written and directed the feature films *Past Perfect* and *Wilby Wonderful*. He makes his home with his husband, Paul Goulet, in Halifax, Nova Scotia.

Characters

Setting

Present day, in and around Halifax, Nova Scotia.

Production History

How It Works was first developed by Mulgrave Road Theatre in association with da da kamera and premiered by Mulgrave Road Theatre, Guysborough, Nova Scotia, on March 24, 2006 with the following artists:

CHRISTINE: .... Mary-Colin Chisholm

AL: .... Brian Heighton

BROOKE: .... Margaret Smith

DONNA: .... Kathryn MacLellan

Director: Daniel MacIvor
Lighting Design: Leigh Ann Vardy
Set Design: Denyse Karn
Stage Manager: Patti Niece
Technical Director: Ian Pygott
Assistant Director: Natasha MacLellan
Producer: Emmy Alcorn

Act One

Prologue

CHRISTINE appears. She speaks to the audience.

CHRISTINE: As far as I can figure, the way that it works is this: everyone has something that happened to them. The thing that we each carry. And you can see it in people, if you look. See it in the way someone walks, in the way someone takes a compliment, sometimes you can just see it in someone's eyes, in one moment, of desperation, of fear, in one quick moment you can see that thing that happened. Everyone has it. The thing that keeps you up at night, or makes you not trust people, or stops love. The thing that hurts. And to stop it, to stop the hurt you have to turn it into a story. And not just a story you play over and over for yourself, but a story that you tell. A story's not a story unless you tell it. And once you tell it, it's not yours anymore. You give it away. And once you give it away it's not something that hurts you anymore, it's something that helps everyone who hears it. It's the kind of thing that's hard to explain. It's probably best if we just show you how it works.

Scene 1

A Bar.

Music: Nina Simone: "Trouble In Mind"

Two chairs and a table.

AL enters and sits at the table. He sits very still and listens to the song. After a moment or two he closes his eyes and lip syncs along with the song. CHRISTINE enters and watches him a moment. She looks around for someone else. Finally she decides it's AL that she's looking for. They speak over the music.

CHRISTINE: Al?

AL: Oh. Yes hi, Al. Ferguson. Al.

CHRISTINE: Christine.

AL: Yes right hi, sit sit. Chris or?

CHRISTINE: Christine.

      CHRISTINE sits.

CHRISTINE: It's a little loud.

AL: Hang on.

      AL leaves.

      The music is turned off.

      AL returns.

I know the bartender.

CHRISTINE: He didn't have to turn it off.

AL: He's going to change it.

CHRISTINE: Is this your regular place?

AL: No, mostly I go to The Duck.

CHRISTINE: I love The Duck. I was there twice last Saturday.

AL: I wasn't there.

CHRISTINE: No you weren't.

             A moment.

AL: Great.

CHRISTINE: Will we have a drink?

AL: I was waiting for you.

CHRISTINE: OK good, OK, I had a coffee across the street, so I'm a bit wound up.

AL: Oh.

CHRISTINE: I was a little nervous. You've got a life-like picture.

AL: Oh. I hope that's a good thing.

CHRISTINE: No it's great. Nobody likes surprises.

AL: No?

CHRISTINE: No. I don't.

AL: Have you met a lot of people on-line?

CHRISTINE: Three. All terrible. It's a weird way to meet people.

AL: Well—

CHRISTINE: I mean and then you get into the whole e-mail back and forth type thing. No thanks. That's why with you it was "Hi?". "Hi." "Wanna meet for coffee?".

AL:　　　　　　That made sense to me.

CHRISTINE:　　It's all a bit of a tease.

AL:　　　　　　You look better than your picture. Not that your picture is—

CHRISTINE:　　No no. It's not the best picture. But I figure, better in person is better right?

AL:　　　　　　Right.

> *A moment.*

CHRISTINE:　　I'm about ready for a drink.

AL:　　　　　　I'll go.

> *AL rises and heads off.*

　　　　　　　　(Turning back.) We're not having coffee are we?

CHRISTINE:　　No.

AL:　　　　　　No. Beer?

CHRISTINE:　　Sure.

AL:　　　　　　Glass?

CHRISTINE:　　No.

AL:　　　　　　Ah.

> *AL leaves.*

CHRISTINE:　　*(Calling off to AL.)* But we can have coffee if you want. I don't need a drink. I could have coffee. I won't sleep for two days though. Coffee winds me up a bit. And I'm already a bit wound up. Maybe decaf.

> *AL returns with two bottles of beer, he hands one to CHRISTINE.*

AL: Beer's good.

                 They sit a moment.

CHRISTINE: I had said that maybe we should meet for coffee but
                 only because I was being on the safe side. Not
                 knowing you and everything right. Because there's
                 a...it's pretty easy to know from just seeing a
                 person in person if that's the kind of person you
                 might want to just have coffee with, which is like
                 twenty minutes, or the kind of person you might
                 have a beer with, which could be like anywhere
                 from, you know, an hour to forever. You know?

AL: "Chemistry."

CHRISTINE: Right. That's me "Looking for Chemistry." And
                 you're "Downtown Nice Guy."

AL: That's me.

CHRISTINE: And you do seem nice. Cheers.

                 They cheer.

CHRISTINE: I'm feeling much more like the beer type energy
                 with you. Are you? With me?

AL: It's good. Very good. Beer's good.

CHRISTINE: Cheers.

                 They cheer.

AL: So you work in retail.

CHRISTINE: Sort of. Cashier. Drug store. But honest to God,
                 they think it's a hospital, you wouldn't believe the
                 number of people who come in there, "My glands
                 are swollen," "What can I do for a sore elbow?" See
                 a doctor!

AL: Right.

CHRISTINE: It's funny though, one time I wanted to be a nurse. But I can't stand people whining. Also I thought it might be nice to work in a bank.

AL: My ex-wife works in a bank.

CHRISTINE: Oh yeah?

AL: Oh oh.

CHRISTINE: What?

AL: That's a bit of a no-no isn't it. Talking about your ex on a blind date.

CHRISTINE: Oh they made it a rule but I only think it matters if you have feelings for them still. Which you…?

AL: Don't.

CHRISTINE: Excellent.

AL: Cheers.

                They cheer. A moment.

AL: You said you liked sports?

CHRISTINE: Curling, bowling and pool.

AL: How about darts?

CHRISTINE: Now?

AL: No. I mean…sometime.

CHRISTINE: For sure. Sometime.

                A moment.

               And you're a consultant.

AL: I work for some people.

CHRISTINE: So what does a consultant do?

AL: Who knows.

CHRISTINE: Right on. *(Sings to the tune of BTO's "Taking Care of Business.")* "Working for the weekend every day, I'm just working for the weekend every way." BTO. Great band.

AL: It's *(Sings.)* "Taking care of business, every day. I'm just taking care of business."

CHRISTINE: Oh.

AL: You're thinking of Loverboy. *(Sings to the tune of Loverboy's "Working For the Weekend.")* "Everybody's working for the weekend."

CHRISTINE: Oh right, Loverboy. Good band. Cheers.

They cheer.

AL: You just moved to the city?

CHRISTINE: Yeah. Two months. I love it. All the people. And the lattés, they're like dessert. Of course then I'm up for a week.

AL: But you're from Jeddore.

CHRISTINE: How did you know that?

AL: It said so in your profile.

CHRISTINE: Oh I just wrote it, I didn't really read it. How's the spelling?

AL: Good good.

CHRISTINE: Oh good. I'm good to spell.

AL: I just bought land near Jeddore. In Mushaboom.

A moment.

CHRISTINE: Oh oh.

AL: What?

CHRISTINE: No, nothing, no just that was a no-no too. That "oh oh." No just I did that thing where you put yourself way into the future with someone, you know, with expectations...

AL: Ah, expectations.

CHRISTINE: Yeah, I expectated us all the way to Mushaboom. Not that that's a bad thing, Mushaboom, just that I was doing that, that was bad thing.

AL: I guess it depends on what we were doing in Mushaboom.

CHRISTINE: Shacked up, drunk and fighting. Which, why does it have to go there right? Or more better, why does it have to go anywhere? All we've got is today right. So we're here and so...cheers.

                    They cheer.

AL: I just need to say...I can't associate with people who are in any way involved with illegal drugs.

CHRISTINE: Oh well I'm not— It's just the coffee.

AL: No no I'm not— It's just a thing— I'm a cop.

CHRISTINE: You're a cop?

AL: Yeah.

CHRISTINE: I totally knew it, I even thought it for a minute. I totally can spot a cop. I love cops. And paramedics, Randolph Mantooth on Emergency? Oh my God. But I was always drawn to cops. Uniform?

AL: No.

CHRISTINE: *(Very excited.)* A detective!

AL: It's not that—

CHRISTINE: Why did you say you were a consultant?

AL: People can get a little excited around the cop thing.

CHRISTINE: *(Calming down.)* Right.

AL: And I do consult. With various people. About the law.

CHRISTINE: Yeah.

AL: And it was probably more the P.I.'s you were into.

CHRISTINE: "The Rockford Files."

AL: Yeah.

CHRISTINE: I loved him.

AL: I have a daughter.

CHRISTINE: Oh yeah? What's her name?

AL: Brooke. She's nineteen.

CHRISTINE: Oh so she's still at home or…?

AL: Yeah, no, yeah, she's still… She has some friends she stays with, she stays with me…sometimes with her mother. She has some health problems.

CHRISTINE: Oh.

AL: No, nothing…it's manageable. More a kind of…exhaustion. But she's coming out of it.

CHRISTINE: Nineteen?

AL: Yeah.

CHRISTINE: Nineteen can be tough.

AL: You have kids?

CHRISTINE: No no. I just remember nineteen. No kids. I was married though. That was a bit of a letdown.

AL: The marriage?

CHRISTINE: That it didn't last. I mean I used to think you could
                    make anything work with anyone. I mean short of
                    a cannibal or something.

AL: You have to want to make it work.

CHRISTINE: Yes you do.

AL: Here's to wanting.

CHRISTINE: To make it work.

AL: Cheers.

                    *They   cheer.   Light   shift.   Music: Fiest:
                    "Mushaboom"*

Scene 2

                    AL's living room.

                    *Music continues. AL enters taking off his coat and
                    turning on lights. Central to the living room is a
                    door.*

AL: Brooke! Brooke! I have neighbours.

                    The music stops.

                    BROOKE enters in comfortable sleepwear.

BROOKE: You play it that loud.

AL: Not at two-thirty.

BROOKE: Sorry. How was Miss Looking for Chemistry? Or
                    was it Mrs. Looking for Chemistry.

AL: Divorced.

BROOKE: And?

AL: She was nice. She wasn't your mother, but we've

	established that I shouldn't be looking for your mother.
BROOKE:	Right.
AL:	Because that didn't work.
BROOKE:	Exactly.
AL:	And if you don't want something to work it's not going to work.
BROOKE:	So you liked her.
AL:	I liked her. But listen, I was thinking about you and you know you really need to get out there. You need to meet people. You need to get excited about somebody.
BROOKE:	Are you saying I need to get a boyfriend?
AL:	Or whatever. A girlfriend.
BROOKE:	I'm not a lesbian. Oh my God. I had made up that thing about Debbie Henderson when I was in Grade Ten.
AL:	But you said—
BROOKE:	I was in Grade Ten. I was just trying to freak you out. And clearly I succeeded.
AL:	OK, you know, whatever, I'm just saying, you need to get out there and you meet people and you get out of yourself a little bit, get into someone else, into possibilities.
BROOKE:	Are you drunk?
AL:	A little.
BROOKE:	Can I have some money?
AL:	I'm not that drunk.

BROOKE: I need to buy some sneakers.

AL: What did you do all night?

BROOKE: Talked on the phone.

AL: To who?

BROOKE: Oh my God.

AL: That's the deal.

BROOKE: Mom.

AL: How's your mother?

BROOKE: Oh she's Donna. As Donna as ever. I had to talk her out of a face-lift.

AL: No way.

BROOKE: It wasn't that hard, she didn't really want to do it anyway. She just needed to be told she was beautiful.

AL: Good.

BROOKE: So I convinced her to go to Mexico instead.

AL: Great.

BROOKE: It's not like you'll have to pay for it.

AL: Oh I'll pay for it, she'll find a way.

BROOKE: She wants me to go with her.

AL: And that's the way.

BROOKE: Whatever.

AL: Which, actually, I would be happy to do. If you wanted to. I think it would be good for you. A trip. You need a change. Right? Would you go?

BROOKE: I don't know. I'm kind of liking being here right now.

A moment.

AL: Are you high?

BROOKE: Why are you asking me that?

AL: Because I just can't tell anymore.

BROOKE: You can tell. Trust me.

AL: Can I? Trust you?

BROOKE: Why are we always talking about this?

AL: It was bad this time.

BROOKE: It's been worse.

AL: It's just taking over more and more of your life every time. You're gone for days.

BROOKE: It's actually better than it was.

AL: You need to get out of yourself, make some friends.

BROOKE: I have friends.

AL: Those people are not your friends Brooke.

BROOKE: Oh my God, when did you turn into a magazine? You used to be this big giant set of encyclopedias. You used to be this interesting guy, with lots of perspectives, questions. Now you're just full of those one-line answers.

AL: Am I supposed to be asking questions, are there questions I'm not asking?

BROOKE: Don't ask me what you're supposed to do, I'm a stranger here myself.

AL: You need to get some help.

BROOKE: I am, I did.

AL: When?

BROOKE: Last week. I saw her once already.

AL: Who paid for that?

BROOKE: It's covered.

AL: Does your mother know?

BROOOKE: No.

AL: Do you want me to tell her?

BROOKE: No.

AL: How was it?

BROOKE: I don't know, she was alright.

AL: I want you to be happy.

BROOKE: Are you happy?

AL: I try. Do you?

BROOKE: I'm trying to. I am.

AL: That's all I want.

BROOKE: So is Ms. Looking for Chemistry going to make you happy?

AL: Nobody can make you happy.

BROOKE: Is she going to help support the happiness you find within yourself.

AL: She likes The Duck, that's a plus.

BROOKE: You went to The Duck?

AL: We ended up there.

BROOKE: What did she think of the Duck?

AL: She loves it. She goes there.

BROOKE: Well she ain't Mom.

AL: No she ain't. And that's a very good thing. Nothing against your mother.

BROOKE: Did you ever go back? To the Duck? With Mom?

AL: No. Just the once.

BROOKE: Oh my God, Mom at the Duck.

AL: It was a first date. I didn't know her, if I'd known her I wouldn't have taken her to the Duck.

BROOKE: After the theatre?

AL: I know I know, I didn't know. I was nervous.

BROOKE: And you were an hour late for the play.

AL: Half an hour. We didn't have cell phones then, you couldn't be driving in a car and call somebody up who was standing waiting on the street.

BROOKE: And she says she doesn't want to go in late and you—

AL: Oh my God you love this story.

BROOKE: —said you oh no no it's fine we'll go in, and she really doesn't want to but she goes in. And the actor starts yelling at you—

AL: The girl. In a fly mask.

BROOKE: And she's yelling at you for being late.

AL: "I am the girl in the fly mask!" God, I never lived that down. And it's all Donna's version.

BROOKE: She always says: "He was an hour late for a play about an insect."

AL: It was her idea. And it wasn't about an insect, it was about a bird. That was the whole point. The fly thought she was a bird so she was one. The fact that your mother'd call it about an insect means that she didn't come close to the message.

BROOKE: And what was the message?

AL: You can be whatever you want. And you can. And you are.

BROOKE: Magazine.

AL: You do look better. It'll be good when we get to the country.

BROOKE: Oh god, the country, yeah. The ocean. That perfect endless everything.

AL: And it's not that far, to get in for a movie or a restaurant.

BROOKE: No exactly. Can I have some money?

AL: Why?

BROOKE: I need new sneakers.

AL: Well, I need some shoes. Want to go tomorrow together?

BROOKE: We'll meet for coffee after.

AL: Alright.

AL takes fifty dollars out of his wallet and hands it to BROOKE.

BROOKE: For that I get one.

AL: *(Takes back the fifty and gives her a hundred.)* Yeah yeah, get a pair.

AL leaves. Music.

BROOKE regards the hundred with increasing importance. She rises and standing centre and holding it out, arm's-length before her. As she speaks to the audience she slowly rolls the bill into a tube. She "injects" the bill into her arm.

BROOKE: Sudafed and iodine soaked in hydrogen peroxide and frozen for half an hour and then dried with a hair dryer. Mixed with microwaved muscle relaxant and matchbooks and cooked at a high heat for an hour and a half and then scraped off the top of a dirty pot. You can eat it, you can snort it, you can smoke it, you can shoot it. Better living through modern chemistry.

Scene 3

DONNA's Bedroom.

Music continues.

DONNA enters in a slip, her hair up, carrying a shirt, calling off. She exits often, changing her clothes and shoes throughout the scene She checks herself in a "mirror" mounted on the fourth wall.

DONNA: Baby? Can you help me? Baby? Brooke?

The music stops. BROOKE speaks from offstage.

BROOKE: *(Off.)* What?

DONNA: Can you do me a favour honey?

BROOKE: *(Off.)* I've got food poisoning I think.

DONNA: What did you eat?

BROOKE: *(Off.)* I don't know, fish or something before.

DONNA: Take some of that pink stuff in the bathroom. And there's half a Valium if you can't sleep.

BROOKE: *(Off.)* Where?

DONNA: In the little wooden box, on my dresser.

BROOKE enters.

BROOKE: Yeah so anyway what?

DONNA: No no honey, if you're not feeling well.

BROOKE: No whatever what?

DONNA offers BROOKE the shirt.

DONNA: Iron this for me?

BROOKE: Ironing!

DONNA: Please Brooke?

BROOKE takes the shirt. DONNA exits.

BROOKE: God, why don't we just heat slate? It's like washing
            clothes in the creek. It's like "the icebox," it's over.
            Get a steamer.

BROOKE leaves.

DONNA: *(Off.)* Get me a steamer for Christmas.

DONNA re-enters.

            But what's ironic is that your father and I had our
            first date at the theatre and he was late now here
            we go again now I'm the one who's late.

BROOKE: *(Off.)* That's not irony.

DONNA: What?

BROOKE: *(Off.)* Nothing.

DONNA: Not to say "here we go again" that I'm thinking
            that that means there's anything special about this
            guy necessarily. He's nice but a bit...nice.
            Although I wasn't sure there was anything special
            about your father when I first met him. He's dating
            isn't he? Brooke?

BROOKE: *(Off.)* What?

DONNA: Your father's dating?

BROOKE: *(Off.)* Oh my God.

DONNA: I'm not pumping you for information. I'm just—

BROOKE: *(Off.)* Yes!

DONNA: Just one person or—

BROOKE: *(Off.)* Perhaps.

DONNA: Have you met her?

            BROOKE enters.

BROOKE: He talks about a woman, he seems to like her, I could probably get her number if you wanted to give her a call. Or you could just ask Dad.

DONNA: I'm sorry.

            BROOKE leaves.

DONNA: I'm just nervous. I haven't really done this dating since your father, and even that was hardly dating. We had the first date and then it was all just...given. And some date. He was an hour late for the play and then afterward he took me for drinks at The Duck.

BROOKE: *(Off.)* What's wrong with The Duck?

DONNA: It's fine for a Saturday afternoon, but after the theatre? You want something a bit less...a bit more.

BROOKE: *(Off.)* The Duck's great.

DONNA: I hear your father celebrated the divorce there.

            BROOKE does not respond.

            Whatever. It's not so much that the dating is different it's just... The rules are the same but the signals have all changed. I mean what's the house key thing? Is it in-your-hand "come in" or in-your-hand "go home"?

BROOKE: *(Off.)* You're not considering bringing some guy back here?

DONNA: Oh my God Brooke, no, are you crazy? No I want the "go home" key signal.

BROOKE enters with the pressed shirt.

BROOKE: Just say no.

BROOKE hands the shirt to DONNA.

And get a steamer.

DONNA: Really I don't even know why I'm doing this. It's not like I'm looking for a relationship. Why else do people date?

BROOKE: Sex.

DONNA exits. BROOKE sits.

DONNA: *(Off.)* Yes well. No thanks. Not tonight. Not tonight honey I have a headache.

DONNA cracks herself up.

BROOKE: Why do you have Valium?

DONNA re-enters, carrying earrings.

DONNA: Oh Dr. Larry gave me a few when the divorce stuff started. They helped though that's for sure, they took the edge off two months of lawyers and alcohol. The end of a marriage.

BROOKE: Why bother?

DONNA: What honey?

BROOKE: Why was it so bad?

DONNA: Oh it wasn't so bad really. It was just…all the lists.
            Everything just came down to lists. All those years.
            All that time. Reduced to lists. And the money. Oh
            the money. Money money money money. Honey,
            what are you going to do?

BROOKE: What?

DONNA: You've got to get something. I mean in the long
            term. For security.

BROOKE: Oh my god I'm totally not feeling well.

DONNA: No not now, I mean in a profound way.

BROOKE: Why does it always have to come down to this?

DONNA: There's no coming down, nothing's coming down
            to anything. Brookie, stay here as long as you like,
            really. I'm just looking at the bigger picture. The
            future.

BROOKE: I know I know. Anyway. Whatever. Yeah. What
            are you doing for earrings?

            DONNA shows her.

            Nice. Dangle-ly.

DONNA: Instant face-lift.

BROOKE: Told you. You're beautiful.

DONNA: No fair.

BROOKE: What?

DONNA: Why are you allowed to say that to me but I can't
            say that to you?

BROOKE: Because you always say it to me when I look
            terrible.

DONNA: That's not true.

BROOKE: What was the play about?

DONNA: Tonight?

BROOKE: No you and Dad.

DONNA: An insect.

BROOKE: No more than that, what was it about about?

DONNA: Oh, the insect wanted to be a bird and so she was and then she died. Really it was about how unhappy the girl in the fly mask was. And angry, oh my God, when Al started talking back and making jokes and the audience was loving it, she was steaming. When she walked off the stage I was kind of hoping that she wouldn't come back at all. No such luck.

BROOKE: And tonight?

DONNA: A little out-there I think, apparently there's lots of nudity.

BROOKE: On a first date?

DONNA: Oh it's the big thing again.

BROOKE: Nudity on a first date?

DONNA: No, in the theatre. And that's the only place there'll be nudity on this first date.

BROOKE: What if he asks?

DONNA: Just say no.

BROOKE: And what if he doesn't?

DONNA: And isn't that the whole thing in a nutshell.

                BROOKE moves to leave. DONNA turns to BROOKE for a compliment.

                Throw me a bone.

BROOKE: Fabulous.

DONNA: I can go with that.

             BROOKE moves to leave.

             Honey, you're doing really well.

BROOKE: People only say that when you're not.

DONNA: That's not true.

BROOKE: People only say it like that when you're not.

             BROOKE leaves. Music. After a moment:

DONNA: *(Calling off.)* I love you Brooke.

BROOKE: *(Off.)* Thank you.

             *DONNA thinks to go to her daughter, then thinks
             again.*

             DONNA leaves.

Scene 4

             AL's living room.

             Music continues.

             *CHRISTINE and AL enter. CHRISTINE sits at the
             table. AL's jacket hangs by the door. AL enters with
             a piece of pie on a plate with a fork.*

AL: Ta da!

             Music stops.

CHRISTINE: And you made this?

AL: I made it.

CHRISTINE: Go on.

AL: From scratch.

CHRISTINE: Crust?

AL: Crust.

CHRISTINE: I couldn't do it. My mother could do it. But to think
                  of my father doing it? Or my brother, ha.

AL: It's just chemistry, and being good with your
                  hands.

CHRISTINE: Everything's just chemistry and being good with
                  your hands.

> *CHRISTINE reaches out for AL's hand. AL gives
> CHRISTINE his hand. Gracefully CHRISTINE
> leads Al from his chair, into her chair, and herself
> into his lap.*

AL: Why, Miss Scarlett!

> *CHRISTINE reaches and takes a forkful of pie. She
> moves the fork to her mouth.*

                  Hang on.

> *AL begins a drum roll with his hands on the table.
> CHRISTINE plays along, building anticipation,
> she takes a bite. She likes the taste. AL finishes the
> roll.*

                  She likes it!

CHRISTINE: I do! It's good!

AL: As I said—

CHRISTINE: How did you do that with the crust?

AL: I can bake a pie.

CHRISTINE: Where's Brooke?

AL: She's staying with Donna for a while.

CHRISTINE: How's Donna?

AL: I told you, she won't talk to me.

CHRISTINE: She won't talk to you at all?

AL: No.

CHRISTINE: Not like "Hi, how are you?"

AL: No no that stuff yeah.

CHRISTINE: Well that's talking.

AL: No that's speaking, we're speaking, but we're not talking.

CHRISTINE: Are you waiting for her to start?

AL: Maybe.

CHRISTINE: And how's that been working?

> *A moment.*

How did Brooke's job interview go today?

AL: Good great I think she got it.

CHRISTINE: Great.

AL: And it's a CD store—and she loves music, also every other member of the staff is a tattooed male toque-wearer, a species she is as of late very…drawn to. So for her the whole thing is win/win.

CHRISTINE: I can't wait to meet her.

AL: She wants to meet you too.

CHRISTINE: How's her exhaustion?

> *AL says nothing for a moment.*

AL: Um.

AL takes a bite of pie. He swallows it.

Now, that's pretty good.

CHRISTINE: The cop can bake a pie.

AL: At your service Ma'am.

CHRISTINE: I didn't know I could still feel like this.

AL: She really liked the pie.

CHRISTINE: No the pie was just the cherry on top.

A banging at the door. CHRISTINE jumps. AL goes to the door.

AL: Who is it?

BROOKE: *(Off.)* Daddy?

AL opens the door and BROOKE stands in the doorway, neither in nor out of the room. BROOKE does not see CHRISTINE.

BROOKE: I didn't get the job.

AL: Oh honey.

BROOKE: I'm totally depressed.

AL: Do you want to stay here?

BROOKE: No Tricia's taking me out for martinis, and we're maybe going to meet up with one of the guys who works at the shop, which I don't know maybe means I still have a chance.

AL: Who's Tricia?

BROOKE: Tricia, you met Tricia.

AL: The girl with that guy Don, with the car?

BROOKE: No no that's Janelle, she's awful no no no, Tricia, you met her, she's really pretty, tall.

BROOKE lifts her hand to indicate "tall". AL notices BROOKE's hand.

AL: Brooke, what happened to your hand?

BROOKE looks at her hand, it is bleeding.

BROOKE: Oh look.

AL: Hang on.

AL rushes off. Swiftly, BROOKE with her good hand, reaches into AL's jacket hanging near the door and takes out his wallet, with a single hand in an expert maneuver she takes the cash out of the wallet. CHRISTINE is shocked and doesn't know how to react. BROOKE grabs AL's cell phone from another pocket. BROOKE sees the piece of pie on the table. She reaches over and grabs it in her hand. BROOKE turns to leave and sees CHRISTINE. Their eyes lock a moment. The world seems to shift. CHRISTINE makes a gentle move toward BROOKE. BROOKE dashes out like a scared animal.

CHRISTINE: Hey.

CHRISTINE steps after BROOKE but she is gone.

              Hey!

CHRISTINE steps away.

              Al!

AL enters with a wet towel.

AL: Is she gone? Shit.

AL returns to the kitchen.

CHRISTINE: She took your stuff, she took your phone.

AL: Oh man.

CHRISTINE: Check your credit cards.

AL returns dialing a cordless phone and steps out the door to see if there is any sign of BROOKE.

AL: She got the credit cards already.

CHRISTINE: You should cancel the phone.

AL steps back in to the room.

Or maybe it's good she'll have a phone.

AL: She'll sell the phone.

(On phone.) It's Ferguson. Who's on duty? ...Give me Bob Walling.

(To CHRISTINE.) There's a market for phones. It's not the first time—

(On phone.) Bob... Al... If any of the boys come across Brooke tonight could you call me first... Yeah...yeah... Thanks.

AL hangs up.

Bob Walling, he's a great guy, he always keeps an eye out for Brooke.

AL exits with phone.

CHRISTINE: I mean I could have done something I guess but it just caught me by surprise and I... And see now there's where I don't like surprises! That's the kind of surprise I get—some people get surprise parties, I get that.

AL returns. A moment.

AL: She's a lot of work.

CHRISTINE: What does she need that she's selling phones for?

A moment.

It's drugs I know.

AL: Yeah.

CHRISTINE: What drugs?

AL: Various. Serious. Whatever she can get off the
               street. She did a rehab—Donna doesn't know
               about the rehab. Brooke didn't want her to and I
               couldn't argue. It was part of the deal. But she's on
               and off still. And I've done everything—all I can do
               is be here.

CHRISTINE: Have you tried not being here?

AL: Yeah but then she goes to her mother's and then
               Donna and I both say no she goes off and
               disappears. To Donna she disappears, and this
               maybe makes it harder but I know where she is,
               from work, you just know, or where she's likely to
               be. And I can't let her be in those places.

CHRISTINE: How she got the gear from your pockets, she
               learned that from a pro.

AL: *(Sheepish.)* Yeah well…

CHRISTINE: You taught her?

AL: It was like a magic trick.

CHRISTINE: That'll make a good story someday.

AL: I hope.

CHRISTINE: And she'll be telling it. And she'll think nothing of
               it, and she'll be laughing, because you're there too,
               and you're laughing.

AL: It seems like it was yesterday, that it was Saturday
               night and we were sitting around the Scrabble
               board. She would have been out with her
               girlfriends the night before, and Donna hot for
               Scrabble all week, and I liked to stay around the
               house on Saturday nights, and also I was a bit of a

Scrabble champ. Which made it fun because Donna and Brooke had this alliance around bringing me down, so they were playing together against me.

CHRISTINE: That sounds like one of those "Survivor" type shows.

AL: Well everything is though isn't it?

CHRISTINE: Not on my channel.

AL: What's on your channel?

CHRISTINE: On my channel is some fun stuff, music videos, movies, lots of movies. And shows about wild animals, because you can learn a lot by watching animals. And anything with East Coast humour, I love East Coast humour. And a bunch of different religious shows, some to maybe watch and some to laugh at, and some to just scare you a bit. Cause that can be good. Oh and Home Shopping. Which I like to have on when I'm doing something boring, like talking to Mom on the phone. And every travel show, I don't care what, even the cheesy ones but nothing where it's about winning. I don't find that fun.

AL: Not a Scrabble person?

CHRISITNE: Oh Scrabble's great, people get so mad. I love Scrabble.

AL: Oh, you've got a Scrabble temper?

CHRISTINE: No I just like to watch. But I bet you've got a Scrabble temper.

AL: No no, I'm very reasonable.

CHRISTINE: Reasonable?

AL: Yes.

CHRISTINE: Reasonable doesn't sound like fun either.

AL: Brooke was a scrapper.

              A moment.

              What am I going to do?

CHRISTINE: I'd take her on.

AL: Take her on how?

CHRISTINE: Toe to toe.

AL: That would be interesting.

CHRISTINE: She doesn't scare me.

AL: She can scare me.

CHRISTINE: She doesn't scare me away from you.

              CHRISTINE leaves.

AL: Then where are you going?

              CHRISTINE motions for AL to follow her off stage.

              Oh.

              Music: Loverboy: "Working For The Weekend."

              AL follows CHRISTINE off.

Scene 5

              A bar.

              Music continues.

              Light shift.

              DONNA sits at a table.

CHRISTINE: *(Off.)* Whoo! Tequila!

Music out. CHRISTINE enters with two shots of tequila, one for herself and one she hands to DONNA.

CHRISTINE sits.

Beer chaser?

DONNA: Sure.

CHRISTINE: Two beer?

DONNA: Yeah.

CHRISTINE: *(Calling off stage to bartender.)* Four beer!

DONNA: I don't know that I'll be able to drink—

CHRISTINE: Oh don't worry somebody'll drink them.

DONNA: So where are you from?

CHRISTINE: *(Raising her glass.)* To Al.

DONNA: Yes.

CHRISTINE shoots hers. DONNA, with some trepidation, follows. DONNA tries not to react to the strength of the shot.

CHRISTINE: *(Reacting to the strength of the shot.)* Whoa bring on those beers.

CHRISTINE dashes off stage. DONNA catches her breath.

CHRISTINE quickly returns with four beer. She hands two to DONNA and keeps two for herself. CHRISTINE takes a healthy drink. DONNA drinks to kill the tequila.

So where am I from? Is that why you called me up to meet? To ask me where I'm from?

DONNA: No. I just… But you and Al are…serious so…

CHRISTINE: We have fun.

DONNA: But you are serious.

CHRISTINE: I don't think—

DONNA: You're not serious?

CHRISTINE: About what?

DONNA: Al.

CHRISTINE: Oh you mean about the future. Like, do we have a future?

DONNA: Yes.

CHRISTINE: Donna… Can I call you Donna?

DONNA: Of course.

CHRISTINE: Donna, it's like this…I don't know.

DONNA: Oh.

CHRISTINE: All we've got is today, and tomorrow who knows?

DONNA: I see.

CHRISTINE: In that, I don't know.

DONNA: OK.

CHRISTINE: You know?

DONNA: That's probably a good thing.

CHRISTINE: All I can say is it's respect and no expectations and trust and good sex.

DONNA: Um…

CHRISTINE: "Um"?

DONNA: I think it's important for me to say that I'm not sure I'm feeling entirely comfortable talking about your sexual relationship with Al.

CHRISTINE: Well that's probably something you might want to
              take up with Dr Phil.

DONNA: Pardon me?

CHRISTINE: Or Oprah.

DONNA: Oprah?

CHRISTINE: All that stuff. But I say at least on "Jerry Springer"
              they weren't always talking from their brains.

DONNA: Really?

CHRISTINE: Lower West Jeddore.

DONNA: Pardon me?

CHRISTINE: Where I'm from, Lower West Jeddore. But I've
              been all over, Florida, Europe, Antigonish for two
              years—

DONNA: You lived in Europe?

CHRISTINE: Three weeks. Bus tour.

DONNA: Oh.

CHRISTINE: But I mean Halifax is great, I love the lattes but they
              get me all spinny. I could see myself living here.

DONNA: With Al?

CHRISTINE: I'd consider that more of a "future" type idea.

DONNA: Right.

CHRISTINE: Are you still in love with Al?

DONNA: God no, no no no no no, oh dear no no no. Not at all.
              God no.

CHRISTINE: Because I thought maybe that's why you called.

DONNA: No no no. Just, I mean no.

A moment.

But there's Brooke.

CHRISTINE: Yes.

DONNA: You've met Brooke?

CHRISTINE: Once.

DONNA: She's going through something.

CHRISTINE: Al's good with her.

DONNA: Just Christine? Or Chris sometimes?

CHRISTINE: Chrissy at home, but just Christine. Chrissy's just family.

DONNA: Chrissy with Al?

CHRISITINE: Not yet. But if it gets followed by "make my dinner" he'll only say it once.

CHRISTINE and DONNA share a laugh.

You like music.

DONNA: Yes. Some. Do you like music?

CHRISTINE: All kinds.

DONNA: Do you play?

CHRISTINE: A musical instrument! Just the stereo.

A moment.

You like Classical Music.

DONNA: Yes, some.

CHRISTINE: I like Beethoven.

DONNA: Beethoven's wonderful.

CHRISTINE: What's your favourite?

DONNA: My favourite?

CHRISTINE: Mine's "Minuet 11." He's amazing. He's got this...
                (Makes gesture of dark intensity.) There's something
                going on there.

DONNA: A dark intensity.

CHRISTINE: Yeah!

                DONNA smiles.

                I love your shoes.

DONNA: Oh thank you.

CHRISTINE: I love shoes. I'm a shoe nut.

DONNA: Really?

CHRISTINE: I can't wear them though, weak ankles and a high
                instep.

DONNA: You just have to find the right shoe.

CHRISTINE: Yeah yeah, that's what Oprah says.

DONNA: You know there is no way that I can drink all this
                beer.

CHRISTINE: That's alright, Al might drop by. If we want him to.

DONNA: I don't think—

CHRISTINE: It might be good, you know?

DONNA: No.

CHRISTINE: Or you know even, I'm totally good to go and let
                you two have a—

DONNA: No. You know what, really actually, I have to go, I
                have a thing later and I have to get ready. I came
                straight from work.

                DONNA begins putting on her coat.

CHRISTINE: I always wanted to work in a bank.

DONNA: Oh it's wildly glamorous.

CHRISTINE: No but I mean it's friendly. Lots of people. Money. I love watching people around money.

DONNA: *(Indicating the drinks.)* I'm going to get this.

CHRISTINE: I got it.

DONNA: Oh, thank you.

CHRISTINE: I'm going to wait for Al.

DONNA: Was Brooke high when you saw her?

CHRISTINE: Yes.

DONNA: Did you know she's been stealing?

CHRISTINE: Yeah.

DONNA: From you?

CHRISTINE: No.

DONNA: Did you know she was in re-hab?

CHRISTINE says nothing.

You knew?

CHRISTINE: Yes.

DONNA: And that is so embarrassing, stupefying, that Al...that they would think I wouldn't find out. I know people. And horrifying that they wouldn't want to tell me.

A moment.

In Grade Eleven she wanted to be a Winter Carnival Princess. Out of nowhere. And that really threw me. I mean people look at me and think I have a crown in my closet, but no. I was never into that. I was more athletic. And so was Brooke, she was a good little volleyball player, tough. And all of a sudden she wants to be a Princess. It was just a surprise. And I don't know if I handled it very well. That's around the time things really started changing.

I used to think she was high if she was lying on the floor, or sick, but I don't know…I think she's high all the time now. She's just not in there. There are flashes… Angry sometimes I recognize her.

CHRISTINE: I'd like to take her on.

DONNA: Take her on?

CHRISTINE: I'd like your permission to take her on.

DONNA: What are you proposing?

CHRISTINE: A weekend.

DONNA: Where?

CHRISTINE: With me.

DONNA: She's actually good right now, she's with me, she's clean three days.

CHRISTINE: How long does that usually last—four days?

DONNA: More sometimes.

CHRISTINE: So let me—

DONNA: I don't even know you.

                DONNA rises to leave.

CHRISTINE: So why did you call me up to meet? Did you find out what you needed to find out?

DONNA: Yes.

CHRISTINE: Nice to meet you.

DONNA: Say hi to Al.

               DONNA leaves.

               Music.

Scene 6

               Police Station.

               Music continues.

               *BROOKE enters in a party dress. Her hands behind
               her back. She turns to take in her surroundings and
               we see that she is in handcuffs.*

               AL enters.

               BROOKE looks at him pleadingly. Music out.

BROOKE: Daddy…?

AL: Yeah I've heard that song before.

               AL leads her off by the arm.

BROOKE: Daddy.

               DONNA enters watching after them.

               (Off.) Daddy!

               After a moment, AL returns.

DONNA: Was that Brooke?

               AL indicates yes.

DONNA: Has she been here before?

AL: Yes.

DONNA: Al!

AL: She didn't want you to know.

DONNA: She can't be making the rules Al.

AL: There's no point in getting angry.

DONNA: I know. Actually I'm relieved that at least this time
                you called me.

                A moment.

DONNA: What happens now?

AL: They book her. She's in and out. But...as of now
                she's officially a file.

DONNA: Three strikes?

AL: Five.

DONNA: Al.

AL: I didn't even know about two of them.

DONNA: What is she thinking? Have you heard from the
                clinic?

AL: She's on a waiting list.

DONNA: And they want her clean how long?

AL: Including day of admission two weeks.

DONNA: That's crazy. Look at her. How can they know what
                they're talking about and say two weeks. If she
                could get two weeks we could do it ourselves.

                DONNA sits.

AL: Christine... Um ...

DONNA: Who is she?

AL: Well you met her.

DONNA: What's this "take her on"?

AL: I think it's basically just hanging out for the weekend.

DONNA: Hanging out for the weekend? What, are they going to do, go skating?

AL: They would just stay at my place.

DONNA: And do what?

AL: Hang out.

DONNA: And where will you be?

AL: At a hotel.

DONNA: You've got this all worked out.

AL: But Christine doesn't want to do it unless you agree.

DONNA: Agree to what? What does she want, mothering rights?

AL: In a sense yes.

DONNA: What does Brooke think?

AL: Brooke doesn't know.

DONNA: Does she have kids?

AL: No.

DONNA: She likes to drink.

AL: She knows when to stop.

DONNA: And she's obsessed with sex.

AL: She's not— She says what's on her mind.

DONNA: Yeah "Jerry Springer" and "Dr Phil."

AL: They aren't on her channel.

DONNA: What?

AL: Nothing.

DONNA: It wasn't like this when we were kids. Was it like this?

AL: Not this bad.

DONNA: Maybe it is about getting her out of the city. When is this house going to be built?

AL: It's not... The house— It's about getting her out of herself.

DONNA: I thought it was about getting into yourself. Finding your strength, finding yourself. Isn't that what it was supposed to be about?

AL: I don't know.

DONNA: Let's just pull over. Can we just pull over a second. Get off the highway, take a walk in a field, catch our breath, have a sandwich. Just take a... What did Brooke call them?

AL: Pit shops.

DONNA: Pit shops. Let's take a pit shop.

AL: I was thinking about Scrabble.

DONNA: I know. I do. That was the best we were then. Is that sad?

AL: No it's a nice memory.

DONNA: Were we supposed to see this coming?

AL: No... I mean, I didn't.

DONNA: And what about Christine?

AL: She got us talking.

DONNA: Tell her yes.

End of Act One.

Act Two

Scene 1

> *A Stage. Twenty years ago.*

> *A GIRL stands on stage in a home-made fly mask.*

GIRL: And now I know, my journey near complete. I am not a bird. I am not an insect. I am the girl in the fly mask! I am the girl in the fly mask!

> *AL and DONNA enter the theatre and take seats.*

AL: *(To DONNA.)* It's going to be OK, it's going to be fine. *(To an audience member.)* Have we missed much?

> *The GIRL speaks directly to AL to shut him up.*

GIRL: I am the girl in the fly mask!

AL: What?

GIRL: I am the girl in the fly mask.

AL: I'm Al Ferguson.

GIRL: I am the girl in the fly mask!

AL: We can see that.

GIRL: Would you like to get on stage?

AL: Do you want me to get on stage?

GIRL: Sure, get on stage.

AL steps toward the stage.

DONNA: *(Laughing.)* No!

AL: *(To DONNA.)* No I've seen this kind of thing before.

              AL steps on stage and looks at the GIRL expectantly.

GIRL: Well, go ahead.

AL: Aren't you going to ask them for a scenario or a place or something? You know, kitchen or gas station. Or is it not that kind of show. *(To audience.)* I always get confused when they talk right to me like that.

VOICE FROM
THE BOOTH: Get off the stage.

AL: *(To GIRL.)* Is she with you?

              The GIRL walks off stage in a huff.

              (To audience.) Was that supposed to happen?

              Blackout.

              Music.

Scene 2

              AL's living room.

              Music continues. CHRISTINE sits reading a magazine.

              Music stops.

              After a moment BROOKE enters and goes to the door.

BROOKE: Bye.

CHRISTINE: Where are you going?

BROOKE: Out.

              BROOKE tries to open the door for a few moments.

              The door is totally locked from the inside.

CHRISTINE: Yup.

BROOKE: Where's the key?

CHRISTINE: Your father has it.

              BROOKE steps off to look for her father. She returns.

BROOKE: Where's Al?

CHRISTINE: In a hotel for two days.

BROOKE: Where?

CHRISTINE: Downtown.

BROOKE: Which hotel?

CHRISTINE: The Westin.

BROOKE: Well I'll call him.

              BROOKE exits to the phone.

CHRISTINE: He took the phones.

              BROOKE re-enters.

BROOKE: He took the phones how?

CHRISTINE: He took the phone in the office and the phone in the bedroom and the phone in the kitchen and he put them in a suitcase and he took them to the hotel with him.

BROOKE: He took the phones.

CHRISTINE: Yup.

BROOKE: There's a plan.

CHRISTINE: There's a plan.

A moment.

BROOKE: And how long is this supposed to last.

CHRISTINE: The weekend.

BROOKE: What's the weekend, Sunday night or Monday morning?

CHRISTINE: Midnight Sunday night.

BROOKE considers this.

BROOKE: Whatever. What do I win?

CHRISTINE: What do you win?

BROOKE: If I make it?

CHRISTINE: Freedom.

BROOKE laughs.

BROOKE: And what gives you the power to grant freedom?

CHRISTINE: A shot of tequila and knowledge of Beethoven. Oh and I told her I liked her shoes.

BROOKE: I have no idea what you're talking about.

CHRISTINE: I talked to your mother.

BROOKE: Donna knows about this?

CHRISTINE: Yup.

BROOKE: The locked door? The phones?

CHRISTINE: Yup.

BROOKE: I find that hard to believe.

CHRISTINE: She gave me the go-ahead.

BROOKE: To do what?

CHRISTINE: To hang out with you for the weekend.

BROOKE: What are we going to do play records?

CHRISTINE: I don't have my records here.

BROOKE: *(For the trillionth time.)* I'm being ironic, oh my God.

CHRISTINE: What?

BROOKE: You and Donna never get irony.

CHRISTINE: You hate ironing.

BROOKE: Not ironing, iron— Oh my God, you're unbelievable, where are you from?

CHRISTINE: Lower West Jeddore.

BROOKE: No I'm just being— Oh my god.

CHRISTINE: Then I did two years in Antigonish. In the convent.

BROOKE: In the convent?

CHRISTINE: Yup.

BROOKE: Wow.

CHRISTINE: Plus a stint in Florida. You been to Florida?

BROOKE: Yeah.

CHRISTINE: Disney World?

BROOKE: Yeah.

CHRISTINE: I was south of all that, deep and dark, down with the alligators.

BROOKE: Right.

CHRISTINE: But you could play records if you wanted to.

BROOKE: I don't have any "records".

CHRISTINE: Yes you do, you have a few.

BROOKE: I have "My Bloody Valentine" and Nick Drake on vinyl. But I don't think it's what you'd be looking for Ma'am, perhaps you'd like to check out our New Country section.

CHRISTINE: It's not "new," what's "new" about it. Its just "Country." There's nothing "new" about Loretta Lynn. Why do they have to put "new" on it? It's like Secretary's Day or Mother's day. They just make that up so they can sell cards and teddy bear hearts.

BROOKE: "They"?

CHRISTINE: Yeah.

BROOKE: Whatever. So what's the deal, I can't go out until Sunday night?

CHRISTINE: Midnight Sunday night.

BROOKE: Oh my God, is this what happens to women who get together with cops? My mother once threatened to get a warrant to search my room.

CHRISTINE: Maybe it's not your father being a cop that brings it on.

A moment.

What happened to you?

BROOKE looks at CHRISTINE a moment. BROOKE rolls her eyes and heads for the door. She remembers it is locked.

BROOKE: Look, I didn't sell his telephone. I just had to make some phone calls. Somebody stole it.

CHRISTINE: You cleaned out his wallet.

BROOKE: I've done lots of things.

BROOKE takes out a cigarette.

CHRISTINE: You can't smoke here.

BROOKE: What?

CHRISTINE: You can smoke in your room, but you can't smoke here.

BROOKE: I can smoke in my room?

CHRISTINE: You can do anything you want in your room. Go crazy.

BROOKE: Go crazy?

CHRISTINE: Right.

BROOKE: I can do anything I want in my room?

CHRISTINE: Yup.

BROOKE: Have fun hanging out. *(Leaving)* See you Sunday.

             BROOKE is gone.

             Light shift.

             Music: Thompson Twins: "Hold Me Now."

Scene 3

             AL's living room/The Duck twenty years ago.

             CHRISTINE sits in the shadows watching as AL and DONNA enter. They sit and lean in close across the table, smiling into one another's faces.

             They turn on a lamp on the table. Music continues under.

AL: I didn't know, I thought it was that kind of show. I mean the mask was pretty funny and she was talking right to me.

DONNA: You're hilarious.

AL: But once she got going again it wasn't bad really.

DONNA: You're hilarious.

AL: Do you like the Duck?

DONNA: The Duck, yes.

            DONNA leans in closer to AL.

AL: You don't like the Duck.

DONNA: No this is nice, I'm having fun.

AL: I'd like to make life perfect for you but I can't.

            BROOKE enters in the shadows and stands near the table watching AL and DONNA.

DONNA: What?

AL: And that makes me sad that I can't. But I'd still like to try.

DONNA: You don't even know me.

AL: There's only one thing I need to know.

DONNA: What?

AL: Do you like darts?

            DONNA laughs.

DONNA: No.

AL: And that's going to be OK.

DONNA: I think so too.

BROOKE: And they lean in and kiss across the table.

            They lean in and kiss across the table.

            Light shift as AL and DONNA leave.

BROOKE sits.

BROOKE: Or she leans in, that's what he always says. I asked her if she did and the way she said no you could tell that she did. She said she would have gone home with him that night. If he'd asked. But he didn't. I think that might have clinched the deal. And Dad at the theatre, ready to be in the show. That's hilarious.

CHRISTINE: Why do you like that story so much?

BROOKE: Oh does it bug you for me to talk about them like that?

CHRISTINE: No.

BROOKE: Because they're totally better off split up. From long ago.

CHRISTINE: But why do you like that story so much?

BROOKE: I don't know it's a good story.

CHRISTINE: Al doesn't tell it that way.

BROOKE: So?

CHRISTINE: Your mother told me an interesting story about you.

BROOKE: What?

CHRISTINE: You were a Winter Carnival Princess.

BROOKE: That was just a phase.

CHRISTINE: She said it seemed a little out of character for you.

BROOKE: I have no character.

CHRISTINE: That's an odd thing to say don't you think?

BROOKE: Oh. Are you trying to "shrink" me? Don't shrink me.

CHRISTINE: What do you talk to your therapist about?

BROOKE: Oh please, she's an idiot. She's on her second divorce.

CHRISTINE: Do you feel like you broke your parents up?

BROOKE: *(Laughing.)* Don't shrink me!

              BROOKE continues laughing.

              And plus that's totally leading the witness.

              BROOKE cracks herself up. She laughs for some time. Her laughter calms.

CHRISTINE: Have you done all the drugs in your room?

BROOKE: Why?

CHRISTINE: Because I'm on my way in there to get whatever's left?

BROOKE: I thought you said I could go crazy in my room.

CHRISTINE: That part of the evening's over, now you've got to go where the drugs keep you safe from.

BROOKE: People aren't coming over are they? It's not some kind of intervention? Like they're not dragging Nana and freaking Debra Freaking Henderson over here are they? And every freaking butthead boyfriend I ever went out with for two weeks. Cause I'm not—I'd go out a window. If I see Nana walk in here—I don't care if we are on the third floor. I would. Cause I'm not.

CHRISTINE: No one's coming over.

BROOKE: Nana doesn't have to be part of this.

CHRISTINE: What's "this"?

              A moment.

              What happened to you?

BROOKE: Now you're just freaking me out.

            (To herself.) Buzz kill buzz kill buzz kill buzz kill...

            CHRISTINE rises and heads out.

CHRISTINE: *(Exiting.)* And I'm going to need to check your purse.

            BROOKE rushes after CHRISTINE.

BROOKE: *(Exiting.)* Leave my room alone!

            DONNA enters through the door into the room.

DONNA: Brooke honey?

Scene 4

            AL's living room/AL and DONNA's living room five years ago.

            BROOKE turns and sees DONNA. Throughout the beginning of the scene BROOKE is tentative, getting her bearings, remembering why she's remembering this.

BROOKE: Hi.

DONNA: Have you done your homework?

BROOKE: Yeah.

DONNA: Do you want me to have a look at it?

BROOKE: No.

DONNA: Just because, you didn't do very well on that algebra test.

BROOKE: I told you, I honestly thought it was Wednesday.

DONNA: Did you check your schedule for tomorrow?

BROOKE: Yes.

DONNA: Good.

BROOKE: Oh. I'm going to need a hundred and fifty dollars.

DONNA: Why?

BROOKE: For a dress and some shoes.

DONNA: For what?

BROOKE: I'm going to be a Winter Carnival Princess.

DONNA: What? Really? You got nominated?

BROOKE: No I just signed up.

DONNA: You signed yourself up to be a princess?

BROOKE: Yeah. They let you now, the last two years.

DONNA: Who else is doing it?

BROOKE: I don't know any of the other girls.

DONNA: None of them? You're doing this all by yourself?

BROOKE: Yeah.

DONNA: I thought you said those Princess girls were awful.

BROOKE: When?

DONNA: Last week at dinner with Bob Walling. He was saying that and you were agreeing.

BROOKE: Bob Walling is an idiot.

DONNA: Brooke, he's your father's best friend.

BROOKE: So can I have a hundred and fifty dollars or not?

DONNA: You want to be Winter Carnival Queen?

BROOKE: I won't win. I just want to be popular. It's just what the popular people do.

DONNA: You're popular.

BROOKE: Please, clearly you have no idea what it's like for me.

DONNA: What do you mean?

BROOKE: I'm invisible.

DONNA: Oh honey that's just Grade Eleven, everybody feels like that.

BROOKE: OK, whether I'm popular or not is off the table. Let's just say I want to be more popular. Look, Grade Ten sucked OK. I am not doing that again. I'm going to try being popular and see if that's any better.

DONNA: That seems a little planned though.

BROOKE: It's high school Mom, you've got to have a plan.

DONNA: I guess.

BROOKE: There's always a plan.

DONNA: Well and there's planning to do. You need a dress and some shoes. How would you like that to work?

BROOKE: I'll go on my own.

DONNA: I'd like to come, and so would your father I'm sure.

BROOKE: Oh my God.

DONNA: It's special.

BROOKE: No pictures.

DONNA: Can Nana come?

BROOKE: Oh my God!

DONNA: Then I'm going to need pictures.

BROOKE: OK, Nana can come.

DONNA: It'll be fun, we'll make it fun.

BROOKE: That would be a bonus.

DONNA: Is everything OK? Brooke? Is everything OK?

BROOKE: Yeah.

DONNA: I love you Brooke.

BROOKE: Me too.

> *DONNA exits and closes the door.*
>
> *Light shift.*
>
> *BROOKE goes to the door. It is locked.*
>
> *Blackout.*

Scene 5

> *AL's living room.*
>
> *BROOKE and CHRISTINE speak rapidly, intense, circling the table. They are lit only by a lamp on the table.*

BROOKE: There are keys.

CHRISTINE: Your father has the keys.

BROOKE: There are two sets of keys. Locks like that you get two sets of keys. There's another set of keys.

CHRISTINE: Your father took all the keys Brooke.

BROOKE: You're lying. You can't do that, it would be illegal or something. I'd have a civil case.

CHRISTINE: Would you like me to call the police?

BROOKE: I'll break the door, I swear to God. There are tools. They wouldn't let him into the hotel with a sledgehammer and a crowbar.

CHRISTINE: The tools are all locked up. And anything sharp. Anything dangerous.

BROOKE: I have to get out.

CHRISTINE: Why?

BROOKE: I have to get out.

CHRISTINE: You can't get out.

BROOKE: I have to get out, I have to get out, I have to get out to get out.

CHRISTINE: You can't get out.

BROOKE: I have to get out.

CHRISTINE: What happened to you Brooke?

BROOKE: Shut up! There are keys.

CHRISTINE: Your father has the keys.

BROOKE: There are two sets of keys.

CHRISTINE: Your father took all the keys Brooke.

BROOKE: You're lying. I'll break down the door, I swear to God. There are tools.

CHRISTINE: The tools are all locked up. Anything sharp. Anything dangerous.

BROOKE: I have to get out.

CHRISTINE: Why?

BROOKE: I have to get out.

CHRISTINE: You can't get out.

BROOKE: I have to get out, I have to get out, I have to get out to get out.

CHRISTINE: You can't get out.

BROOKE: I have to get out.

CHRISTINE: What happened to you Brooke?

BROOKE: Shut up!

                 Blackout.

Scene 6

                 AL's living room. Hours later/AL and DONNA's basement, six years ago.

                 BROOKE and CHRISTINE sit, spent, exhausted.

BROOKE: And now I'm going to crash.

CHRISTINE: You crashed about an hour ago.

BROOKE: How would you know?

CHRISTINE: I know a lot of people.

BROOKE: Not the people I know.

CHRISTINE: What do you think we were up to at to at the convent, making candles? Knitting mittens? We were out, in the world, with the people. I know lots of people, lots of people like you.

BROOKE: You can't shrink me, OK? I'm unshrinkable OK. I'm not even here.

CHRISTINE: What happened to you?

BROOKE: Nothing. How long 'til I can get out of here?

CHRISTINE: Thirty-two hours.

BROOKE: That's just cruel.

CHRISTINE: Are you surprised that I was in the convent?

BROOKE: Not anymore.

CHRISTINE: It was good to have done it, good to have been there. But I came to see I was only there to fix myself. That was before I realized it had nothing to do with myself.

BROOKE: So does it have to do with, "them"?

CHRISTINE: You.

BROOKE: Me?

CHRISTINE: No "You." The thing you feel when somebody says "you to you. "You." "You" is what's alive. The "self" that's just something for making money and buying things. And killing.

BROOKE: What religion is this?

CHRISTINE: No religion. Just Humanity. Ego. The World.

BROOKE: How much longer?

CHRISTINE: Thirty-two hours.

BROOKE: No, thirty-one hours and something!

CHRISTINE: Now I'm being accurate, last time I was splitting the difference.

BROOKE: I want to die.

CHRISTINE: Do you want me to put on your record?

             A moment.

BROOKE: Yeah.

             CHRISTINE exits.

             Music: Nick Drake: "Place To Be."

             BROOKE takes a pillow and lies on the floor.

             CHRISTINE enters with a blanket that she places over BROOKE. CHRISTINE exits.

Light shift.

After a moment AL enters and watches as BROOKE sleeps on the floor.

AL: Brooke?

Music ends. Light shift.

BROOKE slowly sits up.

BROOKE: Hi.

AL: Why do you always end up sleeping in the basement whenever we have a party?

BROOKE: Do I?

AL: If we get too loud just come and tell us to shut up.

BROOKE: No I know.

AL: I didn't even know you went to bed. Everybody was gone by twelve. Usually you're not even home by then on a Friday night.

BROOKE: I forgot you were having the party.

AL: You like the parties.

BROOKE: They can be fun.

AL: I saw you were drinking last night.

BROOKE: I had like a beer or something.

AL: Look, I remember what fifteen was like OK. I know what kids your age are up to. And I know it's different now, it's harder now in some ways.

BROOKE: Oh my God please, I honestly totally had maybe one beer.

AL: You were talking to Bob Walling for a while.

BROOKE: Yeah.

AL: Did you ever figure out if you knew his son?

BROOKE: Yeah. I didn't know I knew him though but I figured it out.

AL: But he's not in your circle?

BROOKE: No, he's a hockey player.

AL: You play volleyball.

BROOKE: Have you been to highschool? Volleyball ain't hockey.

AL: No that's true I guess. What were you and Bob talking about?

               A moment.

BROOKE: How I'm enjoying Grade Ten.

AL: Oh yeah, his wife taught Grade Ten.

BROOKE: Yeah.

AL: That was hard on him. She was sick for a long time. He doesn't talk about it much. Did he talk to you about that?

BROOKE: Once before I think.

AL: He's a good guy, don't you think, Bob Walling?

BROOKE: He's your friend.

AL: But in your estimation?

BROOKE: Yeah sure. He's very charming. He says we have chemistry.

AL: What does that mean?

BROOKE: He has a way with people.

AL: Are you OK?

BROOKE: I think I should probably take this opportunity to tell you that I'm a lesbian.

AL: What?

BROOKE: I'm a lesbian. Debbie Henderson and I are in love.

AL: Oh. OK.

AL sits down.

Are— Do— Is— Does your Mother know?

BROOKE: Hello?

AL: Are you going to tell her?

BROOKE: Hardly.

AL: I mean at some point you'll have to, if you're serious about this.

BROOKE: "If I'm serious about it?" What do you think, it's just a phase? God, typical. Everything's reduced to "growing up." This is who I am. It's not a phase.

AL: So you'll have to talk to your Mother about it.

BROOKE: You tell her.

AL: You want me to tell her?

BROOKE: It's up to you, because I'm not going to tell her.

AL: Let's just see how it goes.

BROOKE: Right.

AL: She seems like a nice girl. Debra.

BROOKE: Yeah. She is. We're in love.

AL: OK.

BROOKE: So whatever.

AL: Alright.

BROOKE: Fine.

             A moment.

AL: You want some waffles?

BROOKE: OK.

AL: I love you Brooke.

BROOKE: I know.

             AL leaves.

             Light shift.

             CHRISTINE enters.

Scene 7

             AL's living room.

             BROOKE does not look at CHRISTINE.

CHRISTINE: Oh, you're awake. You got a good eight hours.

             A moment.

             Are you feeling sick?

             BROOKE shrugs her shoulders.

             You want some peanut butter?

             BROOKE shakes her head "no."

             Do you want to get out?

BROOKE: What?

CHRISTINE: Do you want to get out of here?

BROOKE: I want to get out of everything.

CHRISTINE: Why? What happened to you?

BROOKE: Why are you so sure something happened to me?

CHRISTINE: I can see it in your eyes, you're stuck in yourself.

BROOKE: Oh my God. What were you doing in Florida, running a prison? Leading a cult?

CHRISTINE: I went for the climate but I ended up staying for the alligators. Ugly buggers aren't they?

BROOKE: The alligators?

CHRISTINE: Sneaky. And mean.

BROOKE: You learned a lot from the alligators.

CHRISTINE: Yes I did. "Fear nothing."

BROOKE: Yeah, I've got the T-shirt.

CHRISTINE throws keys on the table.

CHRISTINE: Here are the keys. Go if you like.

BROOKE sits up a moment.

But going's not getting out. Not the kind of getting out you want to do. I'm giving you an option. You can go now continue to live this way, with this misery, this shame. Or you can tell me what happened.

BROOKE looks at CHRISTINE.

BROOKE: How do you know—

CHRISTINE: I know. Like recognizes like.

BROOKE: What difference does it make now?

CHRISTINE: To be free of it?

A moment.

BROOKE: Just by saying it I'll be free of it?

CHRISTINE: It'll start. What happened to you?

BROOKE: They were so happy. I could have said something but I didn't want to mess things up with them. I didn't want it to come between them. But I guess it didn't matter whether or not I said anything. Just the fact that it happened was always there.

CHRISTINE: What happened?

> *BROOKE drops her head in shame. CHRISTINE moves to her and holds her.*
>
> *Blackout.*

Scene 8

> *AL's living room.*
>
> *CHRISTINE sits lit by a single light. BROOKE, in silhouette stands near the door.*

CHRISTINE: I was married to Jesus Christ. That was my first marriage. And it didn't work out and that's my fault. He was great, always kindness, he never raised his voice unless it was through the vanity of a red-faced preacher, and he only wanted what was best for me. You can't beat that. But I realized—as many young brides do—that I had only gotten married to fix myself, to make everything better, so I wouldn't be scared anymore. And things were better in some ways but I was still broken and I was still scared. So I went as far away as I could afford and I ended up in Florida, deep Florida, away from the tourists, in among the alligators. I would wake up in the morning and find alligators in my back yard. I was more than scared now, I was terrified. At night I was sure I could hear them thumping up against the patio doors. And one night, lying in bed, in my terror, I remembered, I remembered something. It was that day, summer side of fall, I was in the front seat, I had my schoolbag in my lap. We had stayed late to work on the yearbook, he was the teacher advisor, it was just getting dark, he was driving me home. We stopped so he could go into a store to pick something up. He came out and I thought he must have bought cigarettes because he didn't have anything in his hands and I was surprised because I didn't think he smoked, and he got in the car and he reached over and took my schoolbag from my lap and put it in the backseat. And the way he did it, he did it with such tenderness that I think I fell in love with him for a minute. And I started talking about whether or not there should be a limit on the number of times a student should be allowed to appear in the candid photos section. And for some reason I knew I couldn't look at him. And then he started and I stopped talking. And I was looking across a field, and in the middle of the field was a tree, alone in the field. And all of a sudden I was in the tree, alone in the tree, watching me in the car. And one night in Florida with the alligators at the door, I remembered that that day, in the cold car I had looked at the girl in the tree and thought "that's good, you are safe over there". I realized I'd left that part of me in the tree in the field, that part that wakes up when someone says "I'd like to talk to you," or "I miss you" or "What happened to you?" I'd been walking around for years stuck in myself, and that's why I was so afraid. It's the self that carries all the hurt, the shame, the fear; nothing can hurt you. Without you there's nothing.

The next morning I woke up and took a boat ride through the alligators. Within a month I was home helping that little girl down out of the tree. And I feel better, and I'm not scared, and I'm a little broken still, who isn't, but now I can feel what it feels like when someone says "I love you."

Music.

BROOKE opens the door, she is lit by the light outside.

BROOKE: I'll be back.

CHRISTINE: I'll be here.

BROOKE leaves.

Light shift.

Music.

Scene 9

A Bar.

CHRISTINE enters the bar and sits.

DONNA enters the bar with a glass of wine and a beer.

Light shift.

DONNA hands the beer to CHRISTINE.

Music out under:

CHRISTINE: You should have told me you were a wine drinker, I wouldn't have been forcing beer on you.

DONNA: No I like beer, it's more of a calorie thing. And I've got this one.

CHRISTINE: Thanks.

DONNA: Cheers.

They cheer.

I just wanted to thank you. Brooke's been different. She's still...she struggles. But she seems better. More herself.

CHRISTINE: Whatever that is.

DONNA: Yes, I guess.

CHRISTINE: She seems happier.

DONNA: Yes she seems happier.

CHRISTINE: Did she tell you about what happened?

DONNA: Just that you were a strict taskmaster. Her words. And she said it was good for her.

        A moment.

        She also told me that you had been a nun.

CHRISTINE: I was in the convent for two years yes.

DONNA: Do you mind if I ask you... Does Al know that?

CHRISTINE: No he doesn't.

DONNA: Why not?

CHRISTINE: It takes time sometimes, to tell things.

DONNA: Yes.

CHRISTINE: And plus I want to be on more solid ground before Al starts worrying about me comparing him to my ex.

        DONNA and CHRISTINE share a laugh.

DONNA: Brooke and I sat on the sofa the other night and watched television. In some homes that would be no big deal, undesired. For me it was so normal it was a miracle—we just sat on the sofa for hours and watched television.

CHRISTINE: Wow, you must have cable.

        CHRISTINE laughs.

DONNA: Thank you.

CHRISTINE: Al won't get cable. I'm going to have to get another job to pay for cable.

DONNA looks at CHRISTINE.

In that, I'm moving in.

DONNA: Oh.

CHRISTINE: I mean if Al's not going to tell you. He wants to have people over for dinner, after the fact, to kind of announce it. But I say for certain information a little preparation is a good thing.

DONNA: Yes. And I'm glad—I'm happy for you both. And for Brooke.

CHRISTINE: She's OK with you for a while?

DONNA: It's nice.

CHRISTINE: Anyway.

DONNA: I bet I could find you some shoes.

CHRISTINE: Bet you couldn't.

DONNA: You're on.

Music: Beethoven: "Minuet 11."

DONNA and CHRISTINE cheer.

Light shift.

Scene 10

AL's living room.

Music continues, loud. BROOKE sits in the armchair. AL sits at the table peeling apples.

AL: And who are these people?

BROOKE: They're nice.

AL: What?

BROOKE: They're nice.

AL: *(Re: music.)* Please Brooke, neighbours, neighbours.

             BROOKE exits.

BROOKE: *(Exiting.)* Sorry sorry.

             Music out.

AL: Who are these people?

             BROOKE re-enters.

BROOKE: Tricia,—

AL: See I have a bad association around this name Tricia.

BROOKE: No Tricia's nice, I used to just use her as a decoy. She was never actually anywhere I said she was. You met Tricia.

AL: When?

BROOKE: At the park with her Mother.

AL: Her Mother?

BROOKE: The blonde with the dog?

AL: Oh right Tricia's Mother, right. Oh, OK, right OK, right.

BROOKE: I'm sure Christine would like her.

AL: Right. And who else?

BROOKE: Tricia's brother Derrick, who's in architecture school, and this guy Shane.

AL: This guy who?

BROOKE: This guy Shane, he's nice.

AL: How many bedrooms?

BROOKE: Four. Oh my God.

AL: Well? And you know these people?

BROOKE: Yes.

AL: This guy Shane?

BROOKE: He's nice. You'll meet him. I'll bring him over.

AL: And then, after, we'll talk.

BROOKE: Fine.

AL: How much money is it?

BROOKE: My share's eight hundred because they want first and last but I've got four from Mom.

AL: So you're short four hundred?

BROOKE: Which is basically what?

AL: Fifty percent of what you need.

BROOKE: You'll like them.

AL: And if so, I'm happy to help.

BROOKE: Thank you.

AL: You're welcome.

            AL leaves with the bowl of apples.

BROOKE: *(Calling off.)* Daddy?

            AL returns wiping his hands in a towel.

AL: Um?

BROOKE: I have to tell you something. Something that happened in Grade Ten. With Bob Walling.

A moment.

AL knows already what he thought he'd never want to know. He sits.

Light Shift. Music: Nick Drake: "Place To Be."

Scene 11

A cottage in the country.

CHRISTINE enters and sets the stage.

CHRISTINE speaks to the audience.

CHRISTINE: They say there's no easy answers or happy endings, they say instead of easy answers there's good questions—whatever that means—and instead of happy endings there's moments. Moments I get. There's only now. Moment by moment. And so I guess I'm probably breaking my own rules here but this, what's about to happen, hasn't really happened yet. This is the future. But who knows how soon it could happen, maybe tonight, somewhere. Someplace downtown maybe. Or deep among the alligators. Maybe Mushaboom.

DONNA, AL and BROOKE enter. As she speaks BROOKE puts a Scrabble game down on the table and she and DONNA go about setting it up. The bag of letters circulates.

BROOKE: And so he taught me how to clean out a wallet with one hand, when I'm a little kid, as a magic trick, and then I grow up and I clean out his wallet with one hand.

AL laughs.

BROOKE: That's "irony."

AL: That's ironic.

DONNA: So not "rain on your wedding day"?

BROOKE: No! That's just bad luck.

CHRISTINE: I heard rain on your wedding day was a good omen.

AL: *(To CHRISTINE.)* I made a pie.

DONNA: Oh your pie's always a bit sweet.

BROOKE: You're a bit heavy on the sugar Dad.

CHRISTINE: Works for me.

               AL, DONNA and BROOKE are sitting at the table. CHRISTINE sits in the armchair behind AL.

AL: *(To CHRISTINE.)* Are you playing?

CHRISTINE: Yeah.

AL: Well you can't sit over there if you're playing.

CHRISTINE: Just to organize my words.

AL: You can see my letters from there.

CHRISTINE: I'd have to stand up to see your letters.

AL: Don't cheat if you're going to play.

CHRISTINE: I don't cheat.

AL: *(Turning to his letters.)* You cheat at Scrabble.

               CHRISTINE stands to look at AL's letters. DONNA and BROOKE crack up. CHRISTINE quickly sits.

AL: *(To DONNA and BROOKE.)* What? *(To CHRISTINE.)* Are you cheating?

CHRISTINE: No.

AL: There's gamesmanship involved here too you
               know.

CHRISTINE: It's not like it's chess or something.

AL: It's not unlike chess.

BROOKE: It's nothing like chess Dad.

AL: Scrabble is a very respectable game.

               *DONNA and BROOKE and CHRISTINE crack
               up.*

               What?

               AL moves to put his letters back in the bag.

               OK we're starting over.

               *Improv   dialogue   under   music: Fiest:
               "Mushaboom."*

               Black out.

               The End.